Property as a Guarantor of Liberty

Property as a
Guarantor of Liberty

James M. Buchanan

Center for Study of Public Choice
George Mason University

The Shaftesbury Papers, 1
Series Editor: Charles K. Rowley

Edward Elgar

Published by
Edward Elgar Publishing Limited
Gower House
Croft Road
Aldershot
Hants GU11 3HR
England

Edward Elgar Publishing Company
Old Post Road
Brookfield
Vermont 05036
USA

British Library Cataloguing in Publication Data

Buchanan, James M.
  Property as a Guarantor of Liberty. –
  (Shaftesbury Papers)
  I. Title   II. Series
  330.17

Library of Congress Cataloguing in Publication Data

Buchanan, James M.
    Property as a guarantor of liberty/James M. Buchanan.
      p.   cm. — (The Shaftesbury papers)
    Includes bibliographical references and index.
    1. Property.   2. Liberty.   I. Title.   II. Series.
  HB701.B87   1993
  330.1'7—dc20   93–10141
                                                            CIP

ISBN 1 85278 733 3

Printed in Great Britain at the University Press, Cambridge

Contents

Prefatory Note

I am aware that the subject matter examined in this book has been variously discussed by social and legal philosophers for many centuries. I am broadly familiar with some, but by no means most, of this material. I have not attempted to relate my arguments to those of others before me, and I have not considered it to be within my responsibility to search the literature for parallel or opposing treatments of particular points.

The reader should not take this book for more than it is: an effort to develop the relationships between liberty and property from a generalized perspective on constitutional order that has been presented in my earlier works. I have understood that such an effort describes the assignment given me by the Editor.

1. Introduction

Historically, linguistically and legally, 'the common or commons' is common property. Several (many) persons (families) share in the usage of a potentially valued resource. Privatization involves the partitioning of this resource among separate users with a specific delineation of boundaries. Incentives for use are modified, and valued product will increase. This simple argument is as old as Aristotle, and it is an important element in the understanding of basic economics.

My thesis in this book is that this simple argument, that we may for convenience label Aristotelian, is categorically different from an alternative defence of private property that has been present, but which has not been nearly so well understood, either by economists or legal-political philosophers. This second argument does not put efficiency or productivity in resource usage in the exclusively dominating criterial role. Liberty, rather than efficiency, assumes critical importance, although these two objectives are complementary in most applications.

A person seeks to minimize the effects on his own well-being exercised by others, whether these effects be expressed directly or indirectly. Independence from the effects imposed by the behaviour of others is a desired end objective. Individuals want to be 'free to choose' among alternatives, and they do not want their choice sets constrained by the actions of other persons, individually or collectively. We may think here of a spectrum ranging from maximal interdependence on the one extreme to maximal independence on the other.

As a sharing participant in the common, the individual is maximally interdependent. The value of the share in the jointly produced 'good' that is secured depends on the behaviour of *all* members of the sharing group, and this value is influenced by the behaviour of the individual only in proportionate relationship to the size of the group. A partitioning of the common with a specific assignment for private and separated spheres of action reduces the dependence of the individual on the behaviour of others, quite apart from any incentive-induced motivation that might generate higher values of product. The liberty of the individual is increased, if we define liberty to relate inversely to the dependence of the individual's well-being on others' behaviour.

Maximal independence is attained only if the individual exists in total isolation from the social nexus, characterized by an absence of even so much as voluntary interaction through trade and exchange. Metaphorically, maximal independence is represented by the self-sufficient family frontier homestead that subsists totally on its own. Hence, the shared common and this self-sufficient homestead stand at opposing ends of the imaginary spectrum introduced earlier.

The efficacy of private or several property, along both the productivity and the liberty dimensions, warrants extended analysis and discussion. Introduction of the second of these dimensions opens up areas of inquiry involving comparative institutional analysis that tend to be overlooked by the concentration on the efficiency dimension alone. The first step, however, is the clarification of the standard or orthodox analysis in such a fashion that will facilitate the ensuing comparative discussion. Chapter 2 takes this step, and, in particular, examines the removal of the 'tragedy of the common' and the 'leap from the Hobbesian jungle' in standard efficiency logic, but as interpreted in a basic contractarian framework. The next step, in Chapter 3, involves the introduction of the liberty dimension and describes a setting in which independence is maximized. Chapter 4 modifies the economic assumptions in order to allow the derivation of a rational or logical basis for a shift from independence to market interdependence. Chapter 5 examines the effect of market dependence on the attitude and behaviour of individual participants, along with the residual role played by property ownership, all of which is analytically illustrated in Chapter 6.

In Chapter 7, some dynamic features of specialization in exchange are analysed, with attendant feedbacks on the dependency status of participating parties. Chapter 8 elaborates a model of competitive process in which the existence of multiple market alternatives, along with free entry and exit, restores to the participant an independence of sorts, but an independence that is based on less secure foundations than that offered through property ownership. In Chapter 9, I suggest that this market independence, as idealized by economists, is not fully understood by individual actors, as is evidenced by apparently 'inefficient' preferences for ownership arrangements. Chapter 10 models ownership, especially of consumer durables, in terms of the self-production of services, and traces the effects of such ownership on individuals' market positions. In Chapter 11, private property in assets that yield money income rather than direct services is discussed, and again the effects of such ownership on market positions are examined. Chapter 12 isolates the role of private ownership of assets in facilitating the accumulation of value through time, and this discussion is followed, in Chapter 13, by specific treatment of the relationship between property ownership and inflation.

With Chapter 14, the book is shifted in its focus, and the effects of socialist organization on ownership, and through this, on liberty, are discussed. Chapter 15 is exclusively devoted to a summary of an early (1893) recognition of socialism's destruction of private ownership to be found in an encyclical by Pope Leo XIII. Chapter 16 discusses briefly the Marxian vision of capitalism as it relates to property and liberty; Chapter 17 includes some final speculations and some Endnotes (Chapter 18) suggest the political-constitutional implications of the whole discussion.

2. The Hobbesian Jungle; the Tragic Common

A familiar starting point for analysis is the state of nature imagined by Thomas Hobbes, in which there is no acknowledgement of what is 'mine and thine', no acceptance of boundaries among persons, no law, no conventions. In this imagined state, the life of any person is described to be 'poore, solitary, nasty, brutish, and short'. Hobbes (1651) used this description of the anarchistic jungle as the basis for his quite convincing argument to the effect that all persons would value security highly enough to surrender authority to an emergent sovereign who promises subsequent protection.

No person would, however, voluntarily acknowledge a sovereign's enforcement authority if it is anticipated that, in the enforced civic order, that person's position will be worse, by his or her own reckoning, than the position attainable in the anarchistic jungle itself. The 'natural equilibrium' of the Hobbesian jungle provides the distributive bench-mark from which the contract between the individual and the sovereign is negotiated. The existence of this back-up, fall-back or exit position places limits on the terms of the contract, as initially negotiated, and it also affects the enforceability of the contract in all subsequent periods of its operation.[1]

It is important to notice that, in this construction, the individual exists prior to, and hence independently of, the contract with the sovereign, even if such an existence is not pleasant by comparison with the ordered alternative that the sovereign offers. The difference between the measured well-being of the individual in the ordered structure guaranteed by the sovereign and the well-being expected in the anarchistic jungle reflects, in one sense, the 'productivity' of the sovereign, and this difference can, for some purposes, be referred to as 'social rent'.

The Hobbesian construction is conjectural and ahistorical. It was not, and is not, intended to be descriptive of reality, past or present. Presumably, individuals have never existed outside the bonds of some collective unit, the extended family, the tribe or the nomadic band. We owe to Hobbes the reductionist explanatory step of imagining the autonomous individual, whose behaviour we might analyse by criteria for rational choice. Such a step serves to facilitate discussion without undermining in any serious way the implications of the analysis.

To modern social scientists, a starting point that is even more familiar than the Hobbesian jungle is the tragic commons, with which I commenced Chapter 1. The formal structure of interaction among participants is, of course, identical in these two settings. This structure is best summarized as the classic prisoners' dilemma (PD), where participants who adhere to strategies that are individually dominant generate outcomes that are less favorable to all parties than those that might be produced by alternative strategy combinations. I want to suggest, however, that, despite this structural identity, the two stylized models of social interaction carry with them differing implications for an understanding of the role played by private or several property, as an institution.

Consider, now, the stylized tragedy of the commons. There is a potential value-generating resource that is used in common by all participants, each one of whom is led, by utility maximizing considerations, to extend individualized usage of the resource beyond that level that would be optimally agreed upon as that participant's proportionate share in an idealized setting for collectively determined utilization. The resource is over-used when private choice is combined with common access; each participant's behaviour, at the relevant margin of use, imposes external diseconomies on the well-being of others in the sharing group; all participants can be made better off, as signalled by their own agreement under some collectively chosen constraints on private choice.

In this stylized example, one implied means of internalization of the relevant externalities is the partitioning of the shared resource among the separate users, the replacement of common usage by private and separated property in specifically assigned parcels. This step involves a removal of all commonality or jointness in utilization of the resource in the apparent direction of independent private usage. In the post-privatization setting, again as stylized, the individual no longer has a utility maximizing incentive to overextend resource use; in the modified setting of private ownership, the individual is led by utility maximizing considerations to use the resource (property) 'optimally' or 'efficiently', since any departure from efficiency results in opportunity costs that are imposed directly and exclusively on the person who makes the decision on usage.

The overall difference in the value of product generated under private ownership and that which is generated under common usage of the resource may be defined as the 'social rent' that emerges from the institutionalization of the regime of private property. In a formal sense, this 'rent' is equivalent to that emergent from the contract with the sovereign in the Hobbesian exemplar. This rent measures the productivity of the institution of private property in the one case and the productivity of the institution of the sovereign in the other.

But something seems to be quasi-contradictory in the juxtaposition of the two familiar models here. The privatization of the commons suggests that productive reform lies in the direction of increasing individual independence (reducing interdependence), whereas agreement among individuals in the contract with the emergent Hobbesian sovereign suggests that productive reform lies in the direction of increasing individual interdependence through membership in the commonly-shared institution of the sovereign. The apparent divergence here stems from the differing emphases in the two models. The metaphor of the tragic commons draws attention to the *assignment* of separated rights of exclusion, separated private spheres, to individuals. This metaphor tends to cause neglect of the problem of *enforcement* of the separated rights, once assigned. By comparison, the metaphor of the anarchistic jungle draws initial attention to the need for some enforcement and protection of the separable claims made by individuals, claims that are presumed established in some prior 'natural equilibrium'. The assignment problem, as such, is conceptually outside the contract with the sovereign, except in application to the rent that emerges from the effective enforcement of claims.

The distinctions between the two models are important in both their explanatory and their normative potentials. The Hobbesian model offers more explanatory power in deriving a theory of legitimacy for a coercive political-legal order from some ultimate agreement among individuals who participate in that order. At the same time, this model also suggests that the sovereign political authority is constrained in its assignment of rights by the set of prior claims advanced by individuals. By comparison, the commons model is less comprehensive in its explanatory power. The defence of private property derived in this model is almost exclusively based on efficiency criteria, and there is no direct reference to problems of enforcement. It is perhaps not surprising that this model seems more congenial to modern welfare economists who have been quite willing to presume that the political authority acts benevolently.

The commons model remains vague on the definition of separated individual claims to shares in the commons, and hence on the basis that might be employed by the collectivity in making any initial partitioning. By implication, the model suggests that the assignment of shares, as such, is somewhat arbitrary, and subject to the unconstrained choice of the collective unit. That is to say, the mind-set encouraged by this model seems to allow readily for the often met claim that the state 'defines property rights'. A more complete analysis of the possible contractual means of emerging from the commons tragedy would, of course, necessarily confront some of these issues. But the very absence of such elements tends to locate the tragic commons metaphor in non-contractarian rather than in contractarian efforts to derive a fundamental logic of private property rights.

Note

1. The argument here has been developed at length in earlier writings. For my own argument, see Buchanan (1975). For other contributions, see Bush (1972) and Tullock (1972; 1974).

3. The Partitioned Commons, the Rule of Law and Boundary Crossings

In Chapter 1, I suggested that a central theme of this book is that the classic Aristotelian defence of private property offers only one part of a two-dimensional normative explanation, and that the relationship between private property and liberty must be added to the relationship between private property and productivity. Chapter 2 presented, in highly summarized fashion, the familiar metaphorical settings that facilitate an understanding of the logic of property, a feeling of how and why private property may emerge from the rational choices of individuals. In this Chapter, I want to extend this discussion and to introduce specifically the relationship between property and independence or liberty.

As the earlier analysis suggests, all individuals who share in the usage of the non-partitioned commons or who find themselves in the anarchistic jungle, will find it in their own interests to enter into some sort of agreement under which the commons will be partitioned or privatized, with each participant thereby securing some assignment of a share with well-defined limits or boundaries. I want to concentrate attention on the agreement here among the separate participants themselves and to neglect, for now, the possible simultaneous agreement between and among individuals and an emergent sovereign. In other words, I want to work within the setting for a Lockean rather than a Hobbesian contract. The initial agreement establishes the boundaries among the separated properties, whether defined in terms of person or thing. For convenience, and without loss of logical structure, the initial agreement might be thought of as assigning to each indi-

vidual property in his or her own person and also some designated area of physical space. The initial agreement establishes
the law of property and defines violations of this law to occur
when boundaries are crossed.

I want to assume further, that, in this first post-partition model,
there are no advantages to specialization in production. Within
his or her own boundaries, each person (or family) finds it possible to use his or her own personal capacities to produce all
'goods' that are demanded, and to do so as efficiently as if
specialization and exchange should be introduced. The model
then becomes one of self-sufficient homesteads, each one of
which operates in total independence of the social nexus, and
protected from encroachment on its territory, including its persons, by the established legal structure.

As constructed, this setting is one in which the individual (or
family unit) enjoys maximal independence and, at the same
time, maximal efficiency in resource or capacity use. By the
prior partitioning of the commons, each decision-making unit
now faces incentives that make utility maximization compatible
with optimal resource usage, inclusively defined. And, by the
presumed productivity of the autarkic organization of the
economy, there is none of the interdependence that is introduced
by specialization, trade and exchange. The individual's well-
being, in his or her own reckoning, depends not at all on the
behaviour of others. The 'goods' that are available for consumption or final use are related in quantity and quality only to the
'bads' that the individual is willing to take on in securing them.
Quite literally, each person does his or her own thing with no
impact on others in the community.

Indeed, there is no community, as such, other than the membership described by adherence to the law of property, as laid
down in the initial agreement. There are only two sharp distinctions to be made in this stylized setting: first, that among individuals as delineated in the law of property, and, second, that
between those who are participants in the legal structure that
defines the separate properties and those who might be outsiders
or foreigners.

I propose to neglect, for now, discussion of the relations be-tween insiders, those who are within the legal structure, and outsiders. For simplicity, assume that there are no outsiders; everyone is a participant in the initial agreement that defines the separated property rights and is thereby subject to the law of property that emerges. The problem of enforcement cannot, how-ever, be neglected if the analysis is to have any claim to logical coherence. Boundary crossings must be expected to occur, even when property is clearly defined, because at least some persons will seek to attain differential advantage through cross-boundary resource use in the absence of an enforcing authority. At the same time that the initial contract is implemented, some provi-sion must be made for policing boundary crossings, to identify and to punish persons who violate the defined property rights of others.

So long as the task of law enforcement cannot be turned over to some non-human technology, elements of the Hobbesian set-ting necessarily present themselves. Enforcement of the law of property requires an enforcing authority; some person or per-sons, whether chosen from inside or outside the initial set of contractors, must be assigned the specialized task of enforcing the boundaries. The presumption of absence of specialization is not sustainable to this extent. And, if the enforcer is granted powers to identify, define and punish lawbreakers, how is this power itself to be contained within desired limits? Who guards the guardians?

The functionalist may respond by pointing to the evolution of the rule of law in some Western societies over some historical epochs. If persons who are assigned powers of enforcement are, themselves, subjected to the same law that they are required to enforce on others, severe limits are placed on their abuses of authority. The complex institutions that involve separation of powers, multiple sovereigns, overlapping jurisdictions, an inde-pendent judiciary and a jury system all find their logical justifi-cation in responses to the question posed. Under an effectively operating rule of law, the individual is protected against the arbitrary exercise of political-legal authority. And, in the stylized setting of economic autarky assumed in this initial model, the independence or liberty of the individual need not be seriously impaired by the necessary presence of the enforcement structure. In this rarified setting, the 'state' exists solely to carry out its protective role, and is, literally, a watchman, night or day. Note that, in this extreme model, there is no need for any role as enforcer of separate contracts among persons, since these contracts are not made.

The stylized model considered in this chapter warrants further discussion. As noted, it is not really appropriate to refer to 'an economy' beyond the level of the individual or family unit, since, by construction, each and every such unit is fully self-sufficient and does not enter into exchange with other units. In terms of our earlier classification, the individual or family unit is maximally independent of other like units in society. The choice set confronting the unit is not affected, in any way, by the choice behaviour of other producing units with which it is associated only through adherence to the law of property. Such independence breaks down only as and if the law of property is violated, either as a result of some failure of the sovereign to police boundary crossings effectively or as a result of the sovereign's own behaviour in crossing boundaries beyond its limits of authority.

I have discussed, elsewhere, problems constraining the sovereign (Buchanan 1975). Here, I want to call attention to features of the stylized model that may be important in shaping attitudes towards the institution of property. How is it possible even *to imagine* a fully self-sufficient economy of the individual or family? Some hypothetical construction of how such an economy would work is required here, a construction that, in its turn, must introduce some imagined classification and definition of the choice problem faced by any such unit. Attention is drawn to the biological necessities: food, shelter, clothing. And we tend to assume that these 'goods', which are universally desired, do not 'grow on trees'; that is, they are not simply available in quantities sufficient to sate all demands. In other words, we presume that scarcity describes the choice setting; the individual or family unit is presumed to be unable to survive without making some internal trade-off between 'bads' and 'goods'. Our whole imagination is shaped for us by the condition of man in some post-Edenic state, man who is forced to labour in order to get that which makes his very existence possible.

It may, of course, be suggested that this universal condition of scarcity is, quite simply, a fact, and that little or no imagination is needed to generalize the condition into individualized settings. I submit, nonetheless, that such imagination may amount to a mental feat of some measure where the relationship between labour and access to items of consumption becomes increasingly attenuated.

I want, however, to go beyond the scarcity implications, as stylized to apply to the economy of the self-sufficient unit, and to flesh out an imaginary description of such a unit's operation. Almost universally here, we would think in terms of an agricultural metaphor, a setting where persons in the self-sufficient unit work *on the land* to produce the goods that are necessary for survival. In economists' terms, the model of self-sufficient homesteads becomes a labour-land, two-factor model of production. Goods are extracted from the land through labour aided and abetted by the forces of nature. This metaphor suggests that *locational fixity* is a characteristic of the self-sufficient autarkic producing-consuming unit. This characteristic has been important in shaping attitudes on the law of property, as I shall note in subsequent discussion.

It should, however, be pointed out that the agricultural metaphor need not be introduced at all. Nature itself may offer abundance, provided only that the individual unit forego the pleasures of idleness and work to exploit that which nature offers. Think of the early American Indians in the Plains when buffalo were superabundant. Self-sufficiency did not imply locational fixity, and land, as a resource, was not scarce.

4. Alienability through Contract: the Emergence of Market Interdependence

Assume that the initial setting is one described by the existence of many self-sufficient homesteads, defined locationally, with private property in person and in land, as protected and enforced by an effective legal structure. I want now to drop the assumption that self-sufficient production is ideally efficient. Assume that specialization is productive; more output can be produced if inputs are specialized. The range of increasing returns is not exploited by the requirements of the single economic unit. Further, assume that this relationship is recognized by all persons.

In this situation, the maximal independence that self-sufficiency makes possible is achieved only at an opportunity cost. To remain isolated in economic autarky, an individual or family unit must forego the 'larger' bundle of goods that might be secured through specialization in production followed by exchange. Autarky involves a utility loss that may be measured in economic value sacrificed. Reciprocally, however, the individual or family unit must also recognize that the larger value promised as a result of specialization and exchange itself involves a utility loss measured in the sacrifice of independence.

If advantages of specialization exist, rational utility maximization will suggest that these advantages would be exploited, to *some* degree. Adam Smith called attention to man's natural propensity to truck and to barter as an explanation of the origins of exchange. But modern economists would not see any need to adduce special propensities, and they would locate the emergence of specialization and exchange in the rational calculus of economic actors. The norms for utility maximization cannot, however, define how much specialization will take place, since independence is also presumed to be a positively valued argument in individuals' utility functions. The precepts of rational choice dictate only that the corner solution represented by economic autarky does not describe behaviour under the conditions postulated. But the individual or family economic unit may enter into the production-exchange nexus over a whole spectrum of economic interdependence, ranging from minimal commitment to maximal.

Analytically, it is useful to proceed in stages. For expository simplicity, let us here assume that the self-sufficient unit allocates its working time among N separate activities, defined in terms of end-items of final consumption, such as growing *grain*, gathering *fuel*, killing *game*, tanning *hides*, building *huts*, etc. For additional ease in exposition, assume that an equal share in working time is devoted to each of these separate activities. Recognizing that there are increasing returns in production, after some talk, members of the separate economic units in a territory, all of whom are within the protection of the law of property, take the initial steps toward market interdependence. A single unit chooses to exploit the returns to scale in, say, one of its activities. It generates a surplus, over and beyond its previously consumed amounts, in one of the N goods. Let us say that unit F_1 chooses to specialize minimally in X_1, by devoting $2/N$, or double, the amount of working time to X_1. By so doing, it produces three units, whereas in the autarkic arrangement only one unit was produced. In this stage of minimal specialization, the economic unit may well continue to produce for its own consumption all of the N goods; the extra time devoted to producing X_1 may be drawn from time spent on all other goods.

The surplus of the one good that exploitation of the returns to scale has generated will be taken to 'the market', in the expectation that other economic units will, reciprocally, bring forth surplus supplies of other goods, thereby facilitating mutually advantageous trades. The favourably expected results are that each individual or family unit can achieve a higher standard of consumption, as measured in more of each and every good, with no more work, than that standard achieved under self-sufficiency.

My purpose here is not that of describing the conjectural history of emerging markets. I leave the medieval fairs and market days to the historians. I want to examine the effects on property rights that are introduced by even minimal entry into the exchange nexus. I shall presume that the legal structure is extended to the enforcement of voluntary contracts between persons and to the effective prevention of fraud in trading.

To the extent that an economic unit specializes in the expectation that a surplus beyond own-use can be traded for other goods desired, the unit is necessarily subjected to the 'blind forces of the market', or to the results of choices made by others over whom no direct control may be exercised. As contrasted with its situation under autarky, in which the isolated unit depends only on its own choices along with the forces of the natural order, there is now a necessary dependence on the behaviour of other economic units. And this behaviour of others is *not* subject to control by the sovereign through laws of property and contract.

Note that, in this setting, entry into the specialization-exchange nexus remains voluntary; the individual or family unit enters 'the market' only in pursuit of the expected higher value of end-items that is promised. The autonomous self-sufficient existence is presumed to exist as a back-up prospect, with own-production of all goods. In a sense, therefore, while entry into the nexus increases the dependence on others, there is no loss of liberty, especially if liberty is defined strictly in negative terms as the absence of coercion by others. The prospect of entering the exchange economy seems, in this setting, to represent an expansion of the choice set.

The positions in the expanded part of the choice set are, however, expectational only, and they are necessarily uncertain. The individual cannot, upon choosing to enter the market nexus, select from among a parametrically-defined menu, as he or she presumably can do within the confines of the internal 'economy' under self-sufficiency. The individual or family cannot unilaterally choose the terms upon which trade of surpluses will take place, and, because of this, cannot choose under certainty the ultimate value enhancement that specialization will make possible.

As the discussion makes clear, the locationally fixed unit that can, if necessary, exist and survive under autarky has nothing to lose and much prospect for gain from limited entry into specialized production and exchange. This model remains, I suspect, the basis of the economists' imagination, and it leads directly to the emphasis on gains-from-trade and mutuality of advantage. The model is perhaps also central to the emphasis on land in attitudes towards the institution of property. If, as we depart from this model, self-sufficiency ceases to be a viable alternative for the individual or family unit, the relationship between property and liberty must be examined in different terms.

5. Market Dependence, Exploitation and Justice in Exchange

As noted in Chapter 4, the person who enters into the nexus of exchange of surplus goods made possible by the advantages of specialization does so voluntarily with the aim of increasing command over whatever bundle of end-items may be desired, even in the full recognition that some sacrifice or loss of independence is involved. That is to say, entry into exchange necessarily produces *dependence* on the behaviour of other persons. Even if there is no coercion, the individual's well-being is subject to change as the result of others' behaviour. And this behaviour will be considered to be variable by the individual who is affected. Hence, others' behaviour will be at least within the domain of criticism, if not of control and manipulation. The individual is 'interested in' the behaviour of others, as such behaviour impacts on his own utility via the market relationship, and in a manner that is different from, say, interest in the ultimate forces of nature, such as weather. This attitude of the single exchange participant carries through even in the setting where no identifiable 'other' person is recognized to exert market power. But the simple fact that any seller must exchange with a single buyer, and vice versa, tends to cause participants to impute market power to others even when such power may be minuscule or absent.

It is not surprising, therefore, that the terms of exchange have been classified as just or unjust almost from the emergence of analysis, and with the implication that some participants, even in wholly voluntary exchanges, may be exploited by others. The very relation of dependence seems to create the potential for exploitation, defined vaguely as some unequal or unbalanced sharing of the gains that exchange makes possible.

Consider, again, the initial shift from self-sufficient economic autarky into exchange interdependence. The farmer produces, say, a surplus of eggs in the expectation that this surplus may be exchanged for, say, potatoes, the own production of which has been reduced by the concentration of resources on eggs. The terms of exchange depend on the number of others in the relevant market who produce surpluses of both eggs and potatoes, along with the relative sizes of these surpluses. If, perchance, the farmer should discover that there are many traders with surpluses of eggs and only one with a surplus of potatoes, the terms of trade will be highly unfavourable. He will surely consider himself to be unjustly treated, or exploited, by the monopolist.

Before entering into market exchange, the individual may, of course, recognize the vulnerability such entry involves and forego some of the advantages promised by specialization by preserving opportunities for exit from market dependency. In our example, the farmer's property holding, in his own labour and in land, allows him to place limits on the potential exploitation that might be generated by unfavourable terms of trade. If all of the resources under his control should be devoted to egg production, the farmer might, in the market circumstances noted, find that he is worse off in market dependency than he would have been by remaining wholly self-sufficient. To forestall such a worst case outcome, the farmer may dedicate a share of his resources to producing potatoes on his own, or some appropriate substitute. In order to take such steps, however, the individual must retain private control over the disposition of productive resources. He must be 'at liberty' to use both labour and land resources in whatever ways he deems fit. Private property ownership allows for specialization and for trade, hence for capture of some share in efficiency gains, but equally important, private property allows for some protection and insulation against the market's 'blind forces', regardless of their ultimate sources.

This second role of private property, which I emphasize in this book, is often neglected, perhaps especially by economists, with their concentration on efficiency, but also by participants in developed market economies where exit options of the sort that

occur in the illustration do not exist for other than a few participants. It is important to recognize, however, that the development of market networks (including futures markets) along with
the accompanying legal-institutional structure, and also associated with the development of an understanding of this structure,
allows the individual participant to secure, in the limiting case,
the full advantages of specialization while at the same time
enjoying the equivalent of costless exit options. This near magi-
cal result is, of course, generated by the existence and operation
of a fully-competitive economy, that is definitionally described
by viable entry and exit into all value-producing activities, in a
market nexus of sufficient size to ensure that there can be many
economic units on both the buying and selling side of any market. In the limiting case, as described in the economists' models,
each person, as a price-taking buyer and/or seller, confronts an
'objective' set of choice options that allows behaviour 'as if' the
interdependence does not exist.

6. Analytical Illustration

The argument sketched out in Chapter 5 may be clarified by an analytical illustration, one that economists may skip over if desired.

Consider, once again, an idealized fully self-subsistent family farming unit, with only two goods of scarcity value, eggs and potatoes. Assume that these goods occupy roughly equal significance in the family budget, or, technically, as arguments in the utility function. Assume, further, that each of these goods may be produced under increasing returns to units of input, in this case, units of labour measured in hours, and also that the two goods are fully symmetrical in the sense that the production functions are the same. In isolated existence, the economic unit faces a production possibility frontier depicted by the curvilinear PP in Figure 6.1, if we assume that the supply of inputs is fixed. Since, by assumption, both potatoes and eggs are defined as goods, and of roughly equal significance, the unit maximizes its utility at E, producing and consuming equal quantities of the two goods. Despite the presence of increasing returns, the unit can do no better than the equilibrium position shown at E.

Note that, in achieving the utility level shown at E, the family is dependent exclusively on its own choices, along with natural forces that operate as constraints. The activity of other persons remains totally irrelevant; there is no economic interdependence present.

We may now change the illustration by introducing a second economic unit, a second farm family, which we shall assume to be, in all respects, identical to the first. This second unit faces precisely the same production function and has precisely the same utility function as the first family. In this setting, there are evident gains to be secured from specialization and exchange.

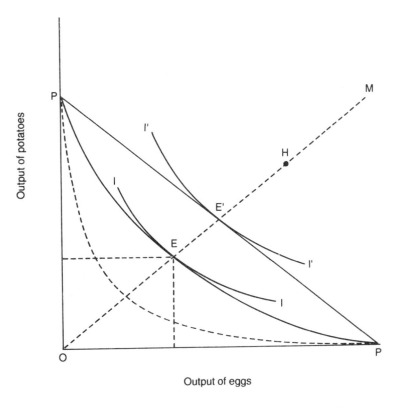

Figure 6.1   Household equilibria with and without exchange

Assume that each of the two units now fully specializes in one of the two goods; one family allocates its total input to the production of potatoes and the other allocates its total input to the production of eggs, with each family devoting the same quantity of inputs to economic production.

Under such conditions, total production in the economy is now depicted in M in Figure 6.1, rather than H, which measures the total product in the economy when the two units produce in isolation and without trade. If the economic units specialize and trade, at an exchange rate of unity (as normalized), each unit can achieve the utility level depicted at E′, clearly higher than that achieved at E.

My emphasis here is on the part of this exercise in elementary economics that economists usually neglect. Each economic unit that specializes and trades does, indeed, secure utility gains by comparison with its position under autarky, but in the process it becomes vulnerable to the behaviour of others beyond its own control. Under autarky, the single unit in the illustration faces the curvilinear possibility frontier PP from which it may, presumably, choose its preferred position by selecting, simultaneously, its rate of production-consumption of the two goods. Under specialization and exchange, the single unit does not face the linear exchange possibility frontier, PP, in the comparable sense of being able to choose simultaneously the final quantities of the two goods. Having specialized in production, say, of eggs, the family has within its own control only the quantity of this good; it depends for its final utility attainment on the behaviour of the other family that specializes in the production of potatoes.

When there are only two economic units, as introduced in the illustration to this point, each unit will, of course, find itself in a position of a bilateral monopolist, with its final utility attainment being dependent on its relative bargaining skills. In this bargaining 'game', the autarkic production possibility frontier defines the limits of vulnerability for the single economic unit; if the other unit is superior in its bargaining skills, the remaining unit may, at worst, resort to autarky, and attain E. In the illustration here, the private property in land and labour, which allows the single family to produce both goods for its own consumption, guarantees the attainment of a utility level not lower than that depicted at E.

The indeterminacy in the solution of the two-person bilateral monopoly game is reduced as the economy, the production-exchange network, increases in size. As each economic unit that specializes in the production of a single good faces the exchange nexus that contains more than a single producer of each other good, its vulnerability to market exploitation decreases. And, as noted earlier, when the network of exchange expands to ensure that there are large numbers of buyers and sellers in all markets, the individual unit may act as if it does indeed face an objective exchange possibility frontier, the linear PP in Figure 6.1.

Beyond the textbook exercises, however, the objectivity of this setting may be questioned. Consider the single person, the seller of eggs, who has within his or her own control only the supply of eggs to be placed on the market. The anticipated price, indicated by the slope of the linear PP in Figure 6.1, depends on there being enough demanders of eggs to sustain this market price for the expected supply, and on there being just enough but not too many other suppliers to make up this expected supply. At best, the price upon which supply adjustments are made by the single seller must be expectational, with its final realization being critically dependent of the aggregate behaviour of many other participants on both sides of the market for the good in question. And, as we know from the historical experiences in those markets where the textbook models of competition have been most nearly matched, the shifts in prices over relatively short periods of time can be dramatic. Any participant who specializes, whether as a buyer-user or as a demander-supplier-producer, remains vulnerable to the behaviour of many others, behaviour which is, to the individual participant, indeed 'blind'.

7. Learning by Doing; Forgetting by Not Doing

In the highly abstracted and simplified illustration discussed in Chapter 6, the vulnerability of the participant in the production-exchange nexus is limited by the availability of the extra-market exit option, as represented by the possible autarkic existence. And the availability of this option does depend critically on the presence of individualized or private property rights that allow voluntary withdrawal from the exchange relationship, either wholly or partially.

The differential attained in the utility level under specialization-exchange and that level that is possible in autarkic isolation, measures the opportunity cost of independence, or, conversely, the benefits of market interdependence. It will be useful to examine briefly some of the factors that may affect the size of this differential. As presented in Chapter 6, the gains from specialization and exchange arise exclusively from increasing returns. I have not introduced the gains that differential factor endowments, including individual skills, capacities and talents, may make possible. The increasing returns emerge because inputs become more adept as rates of output increase, and this relationship may well be accentuated as we move beyond a static to a dynamic model. As production is organized with specialized inputs, participants supplying those inputs learn by doing, and the rate at which inputs are transformed into outputs increases as learning takes place over time.

Economists have recognized that learning by doing is an important element in explanatory models of economic growth. But, to my knowledge, they have not fully incorporated the converse relationship into their analytical models. Participants who specialize in particular activities learn by doing; they become increasingly productive in the activities in which they have chosen to specialize. But they also *forget by not doing*; they become less and less productive in those activities from which they have withdrawn inputs in order to specialize. We may depict this effect in the geometry of the figure used in Chapter 6, Figure 6.1, by indicating that, as the economic units specialize over a sequence of periods, learning by doing and its necessary complement, forgetting by not doing, the extra-market production possibility frontier shifts inward, as shown by the dotted curvilinear line PP. The individual economic unit becomes increasingly dependent upon, and hence vulnerable to, market forces that are beyond its own control. The differential in utility level attainable under specialization and that attainable in autarky increases over time; the extra-market exit option becomes increasingly costly to exercise.

The limits to this dynamic sequence are reached, of course, when the single specialized economic unit has totally forgotten how to, or becomes incompetent to, produce goods other than those for which it is specialized. In our family farm example, suppose that the family unit that specializes in eggs gradually loses all knowledge and capacities that are required to produce potatoes. In this limit, the extra-market exit option takes on a different form. In terms of the geometry of Figure 6.1, the non-market production possibility frontier would now be traced out by the horizontal and vertical axes inside of the Ps on the abscissa and ordinate. Autarkic existence would require continued specialization in one of the two goods, which would be available only for own or internal consumption. The attainable utility level would be that which could be reached at one of the production corners. And this level of utility may not be sufficient to ensure survival and subsistence, especially if the specialization of inputs is on the production of a good that is not sufficiently basic to be counted as a general consumable. The economic unit becomes, in this case, totally dependent on the market's ability to purchase that upon which it specialized, and the only input that can be supplied at all.

8. Private Property, Market Competition and Freedom of Entry and Exit

The limiting case described for the simple analytical illustration in the previous chapters would seem to be applicable for almost all participants in the complex modern economy, where specialization has long been extended to the point where very few, if indeed any at all, families could subsist in extra-market, isolated autarky. Each and every participant, or participating unit, in the modern economy must depend on the behaviour of other persons and units in the system, as organized through markets or otherwise, both to supply the necessary end-items for consumption usage and to demand or purchase the goods and/or services supplied by that single participant or unit.

If extra-market autonomy is not feasible, what protection against potential exploitation is provided by legally guaranteed property rights? Consider, now, the setting in which each participant holds a property right in his or her own person. (We may disregard, for now, private rights in non-human assets.) There are no slaves, and each person remains at liberty to supply those goods or services available to whomever he or she chooses and upon mutually-agreed terms. Absent the autarkic exit option, however, what is the value of this property right?

If there is only one prospective buyer-demander, that is, if a person confronts a monopsonist, the property right to person may, indeed, be of relatively little value. The individual must, somehow, secure access to necessary end-items of consumption in order to subsist, and the monopsonist buyer of the services that can be supplied may extract these on terms that are highly unfavorable to the person who supplies them. But the individual participant need not be put in the position of confronting only a single prospective buyer if the market is organized competitively and is large enough to ensure the presence of multiple buyers and sellers in the markets for all goods and services. In this latter case, the value of the property right in one's own person, as expressed in the liberty to choose among alternative buyers is measured by the full amount of the goods (purchasing power) received in exchange.

(Consider, by contrast with the competitive market setting, that of a socialist regime, where the collectivity owns all means of production. In this situation, each individual who supplies productive services confronts only the single purchaser, the collectivity, and any liberty to choose among alternative purchasers, even if nominally within the individual's possession, becomes almost valueless.)

It is relatively easy to define a market environment in which each participant is confronted with multiple alternatives (buyers-sellers), hence ensuring that the property right to person has maximal value, as this right might be potentially exercised. It is, however, more difficult to describe the institutional rules that encourage the emergence of the competitive environment that is so attractive when defined. Suppose, for example, that all persons in an economy are granted liberty to utilize their personal capacities as they see fit; they are free to choose among any options that appear before them. What is there to ensure that there will be multiple opportunities among which choices are possible?

In order to ensure the emergence and maintenance of a competitive market environment in this sense, individuals must also be allowed the liberty to enter into association, one with another, for the purpose of organizing production units, business firms, which can implement exchanges with persons and other firms. That is to say, individuals must not only be allowed the liberty, as sellers-suppliers, of marketing their own services freely; they must also be allowed the liberty of becoming 'traders' in the grander sense of organizing units that produce and supply goods and services that will ultimately exchange for those services supplied by persons in their individualized capacities.

The economic position of the supplier of productive services is protected by the potential exercise of two complementing sets of property rights. The individual's right to his own person allows him to choose among alternative purchasers of his or her services. It also allows *any* participant to attempt to become a purchaser. Together, these rights operate so as to guarantee severe limits on potential exploitation of the individual through unfavourable terms of trade. The individual supplier retains the right to *exit* from the exchange relationship with any purchaser, and any other individual retains the right to *enter* into an exchange with the individual who sells productive services.

The supplementary condition that is necessary for a competitive market environment, beyond those of free exit and entry, is that the effective size of the exchange nexus be sufficiently large so as to make viable the simultaneous existence of multiple buyers and sellers in each market. This condition may be met, at least in large part, by rules that keep all markets *open* to all potential traders, whether as suppliers or demanders, both those who may be members of the polity and foreigners. Even in markets that may be relatively small, as defined geographically and by membership in a political unit, openness will fix limits on potential abuses of market power by buyers and/or sellers of goods and services that can, either directly or indirectly, be moved across space.

I have suggested that, in the complex modern economy, few, if any, participants can subsist in autarky. An extension of the analytical illustration introduced earlier may have been taken to imply that all participants tend to become narrowly specialized to the production of a single good or service. Such an implication does not, of course, follow, and the disappearance of the autarkic exit option may occur without any such narrow specialization. The individual participant may remain wholly dependent on some market purchase of his or her services, but, at the same time, need not be specialized narrowly to the production of any particular product. This potential substitutability in production serves to make the requirements of effectively competitive markets less restrictive than the earlier discussion might have made them seem. The right to exit from the exchange with any single purchaser allows the participant-supplier to shift among as well as within occupational, industrial and locational categories. Recognition of the enhanced value of the right to exit when the set of options is expanded may cause participants, when considering investing in the human capital required for becoming specialized, to maintain some preferred level of potential flexibility in their productive service capacities.

In the discussion of the minimal requirements of a competitive structure to ensure that liberty in one's own person has significant economic value, I have concentrated on the input or the supply side of the individual's market participation. The individual enters exchange in order to sell his or her productive capacities for money, with which he or she expects to be able to purchase end-items of consumption. Protection against exploitation through manipulation of the terms of trade is provided by the liberty to choose among alternative purchasers, and the competitive process that acts to ensure that alternative purchasers are available at relatively low costs of search and shift.

In some formal sense, the requirements for competition on the demand or output side of an individual's market participation are fully symmetrical with those on the supply side. As a prospective buyer of final end-items, or outputs, the individual is vulnerable to terms-of-trade manipulation unless he or she has the liberty of choosing among alternative sellers along with the availability of such alternatives. But the potential for exploitation on this side of the market is given less attention, properly so, because specialization in consumption rarely extends to the limits of specialization in production. Even if the individual retains the capacity to offer productive services suitable for any of several occupational or industrial categories, once a choice is made, he or she normally supplies inputs to only one purchaser at a time. Rarely do we find persons who work part-time as a carpenter, part-time as a plumber and part-time as a professor of economics. On the demand side, however, such a pattern of consumption is standard behaviour. The individual spends his or her income on a whole set of goods and services, and several goods are consumed or used simultaneously and in mutually complementary ways. The individual is necessarily less dependent on the market structure of supply for any one of the several goods and services in his consumption bundle than he or she is on the market structure of demand for whatever productive services he or she supplies in order to earn income.

This difference in the individual participant's potential vulnerability on the two sides of the market process does not imply that maintenance of an effectively competitive structure is unimportant in markets for consumption goods. The implication is only that the individual's freedom to choose among alternative sellers of goods and services is, in itself, somewhat more efficacious on the demand side, because of the greater substitutability of end-items in the individual's consumption pattern. By inference, the institutional or structural requirements needed to ensure the effectiveness of this freedom to choose become somewhat less critical than the supply side. To introduce a homely example, to the academician, monopsony control over all institutions of higher education and research is more damaging than monopoly control over all the suppliers of bread. It is easier to shift from bread to beans, than it is to shift from being a professor to being a plumber.

9. Professional and Private Images of Markets

Once an understanding of the logical structure of a competitive market economy is fully attained, its aesthetic attractiveness may emerge to render any evaluative judgement suspect. The idealization of the market, that interaction setting in which persons remain maximally interdependent yet where no person exerts arbitrary power over another, becomes a strong normative influence on the way that we interpret that which we can observe directly. And this romanticized interpretation may conflict with other images. The effect is to create an intellectual empty space between the professional economists' model of competitive order and the order that may be indirectly inferred from individuals' behaviour towards private property.

As emphasized in earlier sections of this book, private property protects the liberties of persons by providing viable exit from, or avoidance of entry into, potentially exploitative economic relationships. So long as the individual remains 'free to choose' among alternatives and so long as there exist multiple alternatives from which choice may be exercised, there need be little or no concern about the descriptively observed dependence of the individual on the behaviour of many other persons through the market exchange nexus. In this romanticized vision of the competitive market economy, at least at a first analytical cut, there would seem to be no argument in support of private property in other than person aside from the familiar incentive-efficiency evocation. In other words, the supplementary argument from liberty seems absent in the idealized model of competitive structure.

The theory of the operation of this model tells us that the ownership of non-human assets is simply an alternative to leasing the services of such assets, and that any choice as between these institutional alternatives should rationally be made on the basis of strict cost comparisons. Markets work so as to ensure that these alternatives remain roughly equal in value. Politicized intrusions into markets may, of course, bias the choice alternatives here (e.g., relative tax treatment), but in the competitive market, as idealized, there is no clear case to be made out for widely-dispersed individual ownership of non-human assets, over and beyond the dispersal necessary to ensure the effective working of the competitive process itself. For example, so long as there exists effective competition among suppliers of rental housing units, there is no liberty-based argument for individual family ownership. The same result holds, or carries over, in application to individual ownership of means of transportation such as motor cars and even to the wider set of consumer durables of all varieties.

There seems, however, to be a disparity between the economists' model of competitive markets and the reality of markets as their workings might be inferred from the behaviour of individual participants. Persons do not behave as if markets offer effective alternatives for choice in many situations, and dependence on market-determined terms of trade is treated as a 'bad' in individual utility functions, as we have previously noted. Even in the absence of politicized intrusions that may bias the choice alternatives, individuals place ownership arrangements in a preferred position relative to lease or rental arrangements for many goods and services. Individuals (families) prefer to own their own houses; they prefer to own their own motor cars, as private property, no matter how competitive are the markets for lease-rental arrangements. I suggest, further, that many individuals will prefer ownership to leasing, even if there should exist quite substantial cost or efficiency differences that favor the second of these alternatives. That is, even if the same quality motor car might be leased at, say, $100 per month less than the full monthly cost of owning a motor car, most persons may continue to prefer ownership. The efficiency gains from increased market interdependence are not sufficient to offset the utility loss incurred with reduced independence. As we observe them to behave, therefore, individuals place a positive value on the liberty of the withdrawal from the market nexus that private ownership makes possible, and this evaluation will persist regardless of the degree of competition in particular markets.

10. Private Ownership as Own (Self) Production

One way of interpreting private ownership of non-human assets is to suggest that this institution allows persons to produce the services yielded by those assets for themselves, akin to our earlier example of the egg and potato farmers. The family that owns its residence *produces* its own housing services through time, it does not need to engage in any ongoing contractual or market exchange with suppliers. The individual who owns his own motor car produces transport services day by day as these are needed.

Private ownership allows the individual to move out of the network of exchange-market interdependence and towards the valued position of self-sufficiency. Self-production directly reduces the need that the individual might have to enter the market as a demander-buyer for particular goods and services. And, in this sense, the self-production made possible by ownership of assets is not different, in kind, from the self-production that takes place from applying inputs outside the market structure (e.g., vegetables from a garden). To the extent that ownership is extended to include a larger range of assets (housing, motor cars, furniture, appliances, livestock, fruit trees, etc.) self-production of the goods and services yielded by these assets also reduces the dependence of the individual on the operation of the market for that which is sold in exchange for generalized purchasing power (money income).

This point deserves more detailed discussion. Consider the elementary wheel-of-income diagram shown in Figure 10.1. The individual at A, whom we shall call A, enters the market for inputs (labour services) as a seller-supplier. At the same time, A

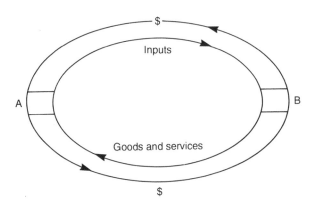

Figure 10.1   The wheel of income

enters the market for outputs (goods and services) as a demander-
buyer. In a fully interdependent market economy, the individual
is dependent on the behaviour of others in the establishment of
the terms of trade in both input and output markets. This structure of interaction was discussed earlier.

As and if the individual at A finds it possible to withdraw
from the market nexus through self-production, the *size* of the
required return flow, on the demander-buyer side of the wheel of
income is reduced. (Ownership of a house eliminates monthly
rental payments.) And, as and if the individual (family) requires
less income flow to purchase the goods and services dictated by
preferences, the need to secure generalized purchasing power
(money income) on the supplier-seller side of the wheel is corre-
spondingly reduced.

The self-production made possible by the ownership of property may be more important in reducing this dependence of the
individual as a seller of inputs than as a buyer of outputs, for
reasons related to, but somewhat different from, those discussed
earlier. Individuals may consider themselves more vulnerable on
the supplier side of the wheel, both because of the relatively
greater specialization involved, and because of the relatively
higher transactions costs incurred in shifting among alternative

buyers, costs that may include locational adjustments. Consider the position of the person who becomes unemployed as a result of market forces. If this person owns a house, car, furniture and appliances, the vulnerability to the market shock is very substantially mitigated. Self-production of the services yielded by these assets facilitates subsistence on much more acceptable terms than would be the case in the absence of property holdings.

Economists should, I think, recognize that the institution of private property presents a paradox in the sense that it exists as a publicly-acknowledged counter to the presumed superior 'efficiency' of market interdependence. In its idealized operation, the market should be able to offer more services for the same outlay, or the same services with less outlay, than that ratio experienced under the self-production arrangements of private property. An ideal housing market could supply persons with the identical housing services at less cost due to the economies of scale in production. (Why should every suburban household own its own lawn-mower?)

The vulnerability of the individual in the market relationship is not incorporated in the standard analytical exercises which implicitly presume that the models work ideally. But the freedom from the shocks that the market may deliver must be entered as a positively-valued argument in a meaningful utility function. In the more inclusive formulation that would allow for this change in utility functions, the self-production that the ownership of property makes possible becomes 'efficient' relative to that of the market, at least within some limits.

11. Private Property in Assets that Yield Money Income

The efficacy of private ownership in insulating individuals from market shocks discussed to this point applies only to those assets that yield goods and services directly, in kind, to the owner. References were made to housing and consumer durables in particular. The implications do not extend to private ownership of assets that yield money income to the owner rather than direct services. Note that the distinction here is not equivalent to that between real assets and financial assets, since some real assets also yield money income rather than income in kind. Almost by definition, of course, financial assets yield money income rather than direct services.

The owner of a financial asset, say, a bond, produces nothing directly that is comparable to the housing services produced by home ownership. Clearly, the ownership of a claim to money income does not represent a withdrawal from the market nexus to the same extent as ownership of an asset yielding income in kind. The owner of the bond must still pay his monthly rent for housing, must meet the lease payments on his or her car and finance the TV rentals when due. Ownership of a claim to money income exerts no influence on the position of the individual as a demander-buyer of final end-items of consumption or use. The potential vulnerability to market shocks through terms of trade for purchased goods is not affected. On the supplier-seller side of the income wheel, however, any claim to money income attributable to the ownership of an asset must act to reduce the necessity of selling current inputs in order to finance consumption goods. The person who gets $100 per month in interest on a bond or money-market account needs $100 less in current earnings from the sale of labour services to finance spending on consumption goods. One way of putting the point here is to say that the owner of an asset produces income that facilitates the purchase of a higher-valued bundle of end-items from the market, or the sale of a smaller bundle of inputs to the market. But the income must, in either case, be processed through the market. By contrast, the owner of an asset, yielding services directly in kind, is relieved of any market throughput, and necessary transformation of value through the exchange nexus.

A further distinction must be made between those privately-owned assets that yield services which are then sold by the owner for money and those assets that yield a direct money return without intermediate sale. In both cases, ownership produces a money income flow that decreases dependence on the sale of current inputs to the market. But there are differing vulnerabilities to forces beyond the control of the owner. In the first case, where a real asset yields services that must then be sold in order to secure money income, the owner remains vulnerable to the vicissitudes of the market for similar earning assets. In the second case, where the ownership claim yields a money return directly, the vulnerability is to shifts in the terms of trade between money and goods generally. This vulnerability is maximal when private property takes the form of money, as such, or in claims that guarantee returns stated in nominal monetary units. I shall defer explicit discussion of the relationship between private property in money or money claims until Chapter 13.

12. Private Property and Time: Accumulation through Ownership

To this point, I have neglected any discussion of the role of private property, regardless of the form that ownership takes, in facilitating individual adjustments *over time* from those patterns of income flows, both in receipts and outlays, that the market generates to those patterns that might be preferred whether from life-cycle or intergenerational motives. In other words, the analysis has been limited to the role of ownership in satisfying essentially the precautionary motives, which would be absent under the workings of idealized markets. Implicitly, the analysis has presented the argument for private ownership in a model where all participants in an economy live forever and remain fixed in their capacities to supply inputs and demand outputs over time. If time is introduced meaningfully into the model, it becomes evident that preferred temporal adjustment to income and outlay flows within individual life spans or between generations requires some institution that allows partitionable claims to values that are realizable in later time periods. Full ownership of personal capacities will allow partial satisfaction of this requirement through the accumulation of human capital, but ownership of non-human assets, in whatever form, is a necessary supplement.

My concern here is not with the relationship between private ownership of property and rates of capital accumulation and, hence, rates of aggregate economic growth in a nation. This argument is akin to that derived from the standard efficiency norm. I do not, of course, question either the validity or the importance of property institutions in generating either economic efficiency or growth, both of which may be widely-accepted objectives. But my purpose in this book is limited to an attempted justification of private ownership as a means of protecting the liberties of persons, quite independently of efficiency or growth considerations.

As suggested earlier, private property, whether or not the asset yields an income through time, allows the owner temporally to withdraw from the market nexus. The person who has income from an owned asset, or an asset that is itself valued, may, if he or she so chooses, either increase current period outlays on final goods or reduce current period sale-supply of inputs to the market. In either case, ownership of valued assets allows for an increase in the individual's choice set. And note that the owner has available an exit option that carries value, whether or not this option is exercised. The owner of the valued asset remains 'free to choose' over a wider range of options, so long as the asset value itself is not eroded. As Samuel Johnson suggested indirectly, the person is most at liberty when he or she owns valued assets that are *not* dissipated (Boswell 1946).

The role of private ownership of property in facilitating preferred temporal adjustment in flows of income and outlay is not directly related to the efficacy of the operation of competitive market forces, as is the case with the precautionary motivations previously discussed. Even if the competitive process is such as to present the individual with multiple alternatives in each and every market at all points in time, partitionable claims to value, or property, will be needed to allow adjustment to the inexorable forces of 'life in real time'. The individual who may express little or no concern about exposure to the 'blind forces of the market', who holds fast to the classical liberal's faith in competitive process, will continue to require private ownership of valued assets.

There are implications for the preferred form of property to be derived from the differing motivations for acquisition and holding assets. For the person who does place full trust in competitive market process, and whose sole or primary motivation is to be able to make intertemporal adjustments in income and outgo, the preferred form of asset should be that which is most readily transformable into other holdings of value, which is, of course, money itself. If we can ignore the precautionary motivation, even with reference to shifts in the terms of trade between money and goods, money or claims to money must be the preferred form of accumulation. The person who finds no advantage in the self-production of services in kind from property, and who seeks some store of value asset exclusively for the purpose of intertemporal adjustment, will opt for the purchase of financial claims with any funds released from current spending.

13. Private Property in Money: Inflation and the Confiscation of Value

The relationship between inflation and the liberty-based defence of private property requires further examination. As noted, the individual who remains unconcerned about vulnerability to particular market shocks will find property ownership necessary to allow for temporal adjustment in income and outlay flows, but, ideally, would choose to hold property in generalized purchasing power, in money or claims to money. Such an idealized setting, however, requires more than the effective operation of the competitive process in every market for goods and services. The setting must also ensure that there are no shocks in the terms of trade between money and goods against which some protection is deemed to be desirable. And this condition is not one that can be met by the working of markets in real world settings.

It is possible to construct an analytical model in which money takes the form of a commodity or commodity bundle, in which case the workings of the competitive market might be expected to ensure reasonable stability in the money-goods terms of trade. In economies as we observe them, however, money is not a commodity produced and sold through markets; it is, instead, a creation of the state, or political unit, and its supply bears little or no relationship to its production cost. For an individual who seeks to hold property in money or money claims, therefore, the protection sought is that against the potential exploitation through the state, or collective agency, rather than against the workings of the market, as such.

The sources of a possible precautionary motive for seeking protection against potential confiscations of expected values are psychologically different in the two settings examined. The person who seeks protection against the 'blind forces of the market' need not fear the machinations of identified or even identifiable persons or groups of persons. The protection sought here is against the aggregate reaction behaviour of large numbers of sellers and buyers, as such behaviour produces emergent results in the pattern of input and output prices in markets. This sort of protection, as sought, is inversely related to what might be called 'trust' in the market process, a 'trust' that depends for its rational origins only on some broad presumption that persons tend to seek their own economic advantage. By dramatic contrast, the person who seeks protection against shocks to the money-goods terms of trade must be concerned, not with the behaviour of many suppliers-demanders in market settings, but with the particular behaviour of agents who can be identified as acting for the political unit. By the law of large numbers, the aggregate behaviour of many persons in markets is more predictable, other things equal, than the behaviour of particular persons in their roles as monetary agents for the state.

Relatively few persons will be unaware of the potential for exploitation by the state through its authority to manipulate the terms of trade between money and goods to its own economic advantage. Some lessons from history are learned. Persons who seek only to acquire property to adjust income and outlay flows through time will modify their behaviour in efforts to forestall such potential exploitation. The exercise of the precautionary motive here will reflect preferences for real assets as opposed to financial assets. Real assets will be demanded neither for their potential self-production of services nor for their measured rates of return, but, instead, for their capital-value accretion as the money-goods terms of trade shift against money. The absence of confidence in the politicized agency that directly influences the money-goods exchange rate represents a restriction on the domain of private property as evaluated in terms of the potential protection of the liberties of persons.

This property-expanding role of monetary credibility is not normally considered in discussions of monetary arrangements.

Here, as elsewhere, economists tend to stress the efficiency-enhancing characteristics of predictability in the value of the monetary unit. Such characteristics are, of course, critically important; contractual arrangements of all varieties are vastly simplified in a regime where predictability in the value of a numéraire exists and is expected to exist. Over and beyond this familiar normative argument for an effective monetary constitution, however, economists (and others) should also recognize that individuals, in their personal-private role, and wholly divorced from any contractual interactions, are made more *independent,* in the sense emphasized in these chapters, under a regime of predictability in the money-goods exchange rate than under a regime where such predictability is absent. By being able to hold stores of value in money, or claims to money, the individual secures generalized protection against particular market fluctuations, on either the input or output sides.

The implications are straightforward. A regime that includes legal protection for private-property holdings is severely limited in its efficacy if predictability in the money-goods exchange rate is absent. And a regime that seeks to privatize ownership of ordinary assets must accompany any privatization steps by the implementation of a monetary constitution that will introduce such predictability, and make it credible. So long as the political authority retains the effective power (and is understood to do so) to confiscate property-holdings that are denominated in monetary units of account, the legal structure that allows persons to own and control assets remains crippled; the potential efficacy of the institution of private property itself remains only half-way exploited.

14. Socialism, Private Property and Liberty

Concentration on the liberty-extending elements of private property ownership offers perhaps a more comprehensive appreciation of the necessary restrictions on liberty that socialism, as an organizational structure, must entail. Socialism, by its classical definition, has as its central feature the displacement of private ownership by collective or state ownership. And, as the domain of activity brought within the organizational umbrella of socialism expands the domain of private ownership diminishes, *pari passu*. The domain of socialist organization is never total in the sense that persons are prohibited from the ownership of any and all valued assets, including the values in their own capacities. Even the most totalitarian regimes allow for *de facto* private ownership of some valued assets, even if these be restricted to precious metals and trinkets.

But consider the position of the individual in a socialist regime in which all productive assets are owned and controlled by the collective authority, including those that could be represented in the individual's own human capital. The individual is *assigned* to a specific occupational, locational role as a supplier of inputs and is *assigned*, in turn, a designated share or quota in the final outputs that the system generates, outputs that are, themselves, selected by the collective authority.

In this setting, the participant in the inclusive socialist enterprise is maximally dependent upon, and hence vulnerable to, the decisions of others, and there is no systemic guarantor against exploitation akin to that offered in a competitive market structure. The individual confronts, simultaneously, a monopsony 'purchaser' of services and a monopoly 'seller' of goods that are required for subsistence. There is no exit option available, in either the input 'market' or the output 'market'. And, holding no value-producing assets privately, the individual has no recourse to self-production, even in any limited sense.

Even if (and contrary to both analytical and empirical evidence) the socialist regime could be 'efficient' in some questionably meaningful sense, the argument for independence or liberty in the individual's utility function would not be allowed expression. Most participants, even in the idealized and imaginary socialist paradise, would prefer, if necessary, some sacrifice in productive potential in exchange for some protection against exploitation by collectivized authority. In reality, of course, no such trade-off between domains exists. Instead, both logical analysis and historical record suggests that 'the economy' becomes less rather than more 'productive' as the domain of collectivization is extended. Only as the boundaries of collective control are reduced, and as private ownership of valued assets increases, do we expect increases in overall economic productivity. But, also, and importantly for the emphasis in this book, persons place positive value on the limited independence that any such shift to private ownership embodies, value over and beyond any increase in efficiency-productivity.

From the temporal perspective of the early 1990s, it is perhaps too easy to understand what seem to be the flaws in the socialist model of political-economic reality. Conversely, it is difficult for those of us who have observed socialism's collapse, both in idea and in application, to understand the dominance of the socialist-collectivist vision in good minds for more than a century, both in the positive analysis of institutional working properties and in the accompanying normative comparative evaluation. F. A. Hayek is surely correct in suggesting that much scholarship will go into attempts to determine why and how 'the fatal conceit' that was socialism could have commanded and maintained the intellectual heights for so long (Hayek 1988).

My suggestion here is that one source of the fatal conceit or delusion stems from the undue concentration of economists on the efficiency-productivity elements of social organization to the neglect of the liberty dimension. If efficiency is taken, even if implicitly, to be the end objective of relevance, a series of related *scientific* errors could have generated the historical record of the socialist century. In retrospect, we may interpret this record as a falsification of the hypothesis that collective ownership and control of the means of production generates product value equal to or even superior to that generated under private ownership arrangements. At least until the 1950s and 1960s, this hypothesis seemed to remain unfalsified. But consider, by way of contrast, the parallel hypothesis that might have been, but was not, made central in comparative institutional-organizational analysis, the hypothesis that incorporates the liberty dimension. Even as an initial hypothesis, no one could have seriously advanced the proposition that collective ownership and control involves an extension in the liberties of individual participants. The restrictions on liberty that necessarily characterize any socialist organization, large or small, comprehensive or piecemeal, were more or less acknowledged by all observers from the onset of the experiments.

15. *Rerum Novarum*

As we review the discussion over the course of the socialist century, we note that the issues were not exclusively joined along the efficiency-productivity dimension. The effects on individual liberty that a shift from a regime of private to collective ownership involves became the basis for an independent and important critique of socialism, and a critique that did not reflect either an understanding of the efficiency argument or even an appreciation of the competitive market process. I refer to the papal encyclical of Leo XIII that was issued in 1893 and widely known by its Latin title, *Rerum Novarum* (1939).[1]

Extended citation from the early sections of this encyclical seems warranted:

> ... the *Socialists*, working on the poor man's envy of the rich, endeavor to destroy private property, and maintain that individual possessions should become the common property of all, to be administered by the State or by municipal bodies. They hold that, by thus transferring property from private persons to the community, the present evil state of things will be set to rights, because each citizen will then have his equal share of whatever there is to enjoy. But their proposals are so clearly futile for all practical purposes, that if they were carried out the working man himself would be among the first to suffer. Moreover they are emphatically unjust, because they rob the lawful possessor, bring the State into a sphere that is not its own, and cause complete confusion in the community.

Private Ownership

It is surely undeniable that, when a man engages in remunerative labour, the very reason and motive of his work is to obtain property, and to hold it as his own private possession. If one man hires out to another his strength or his energy, he does this for the purpose of receiving in return what is necessary for food and living; he thereby expressly proposes to acquire a full and real right, not only to the remuneration, but also to the disposal of that remuneration as he pleases. Thus, if he lives sparingly, saves money, and invests his savings, for greater security, in land, the land in such a case is only his wages in another form; and, consequently, a working man's little estate thus purchased should be as completely at his own disposal as the wages he receives for his labour. But it is precisely in this power of disposal that ownership consists, whether the property be land or movable goods. The *Socialists,* therefore, in endeavoring to transfer the possessions of individuals to the community, strike at the interests of every wage earner, for they deprive him of the liberty of disposing of his wages, and thus of all hope and possibility of increasing his stock and of bettering his condition in life. (pp. 2–3)

... it must be within his (man's) right to have things not merely for temporary and momentary use, as other living beings have them, but in stable and permanent possession; he must have not only things that perish in the using, but also those that, though used, remain for use in the future. (p. 3)

...

And to say that God has given the earth to the use and enjoyment of the universal human race is not to deny that there can be private property. For God has granted the earth to mankind in general; not in the sense that all without distinction can deal with it as they please, but rather that no part of it has been assigned to any one in particular, and that the limits of private possession have been left to be fixed by man's own industry and the laws of individual peoples. (p. 4)

... We are told that it is right for private persons to have the use of the soil and the fruits of their land, but that it is unjust for anyone to possess as owner either the land on which he has built or the estate which he has cultivated. But those who assert this do not perceive that they are robbing man of what his own labour has produced, for the soil which is tilled and cultivated with toil and skill utterly changes its condition; it was wild before, it is now fruitful; it was barren, now it brings forth in abundance. That which has thus altered and improved it becomes so truly a part of itself as to be in a great measure indistinguishable, inseparable from it. Is it just that the fruit of man's sweat and labour should be enjoyed by another?

These statements from *Rerum Novarum* may be interpreted, I think naively, as simple assertions to the effect that persons have natural rights to own separable properties, rights that are independent of any assessment of the relative productivity or efficiency of private and state ownership arrangements. A more careful reading suggests that the author(s) of these passages understood the intimate relationship between individual rights of property ownership and liberty. The empirical proposition is that individuals desire ownership of property in order to secure and to maintain the liberty over the disposal of resources, without which liberty there could be no hope of bettering the conditions of life.

Note that the hope of betterment is individualized. The individual may, if secure in a regime that allows the acquisition of property, along with the maintenance and increase in value through time, *on his own account,* better his condition, and quite independently of any complementing collective action, beyond that required for the necessary functioning of the legal order. Note that there is no consideration at all given to the prospect that the betterment of the working man's condition may be achieved through collective or community ownership. Implicitly, *Rerum Novarum's* defence of private property embodies a recognition of the value persons place on the independence that only a private ownership regime can offer.

Note

1. This encyclical was first called to my attention by Michael Novak, American Enterprise Institute.

16. The Marxian Proletariat and Malthusian Prophecy

The passages from *Rerum Novarum* in Chapter 15 make it clear that the right to own property is the means through which workers can better their own condition. Implicit in the whole discussion there is the denial of classical economists' cost-of-production theory of wages. In order for the acquisition of property to be a meaningful objective for workers, wages must be more than sufficient to ensure survival at a mere subsistence level that allows only for the reproduction of labour. In the Marxian extension of classical economics, workers remain unable to achieve the minimal liberty that property ownership makes possible; workers remain trapped within the industrial proletariat, subject to the inexorable operation of the capitalist production process that necessarily directs all of the economic surplus to the capitalist owners of the non-labour means of production. Workers are maximally vulnerable to the 'blind forces of the market' which ensure their exploitation independently of any failure or breakdown of the market process itself. In this Marxian model of industrial capitalism, workers cannot acquire the property that could offer even a partial exit option from the economic nexus, and any ability to choose among alternative buyers for their labour services offers no in-market analogue since the exploitation is in no sense imputable to particular employers.

The Marxian failure to escape the intellectual strait-jacket imposed by the classical theory of distribution reflected itself in a blindness to the potential equilibrating activity of entrepreneurs who emerge to seek profit from any differential between the productive value of labour and the level of wages. An understanding of the competitive market process would have suggested that, even if the Malthusian prophecy concerning rates of population increase holds, workers would, in all periods prior to the ultimate, and quite dismal, stationary state, find property acquisition possible. Nonetheless, the Malthusian devil would operate over time to reduce the viability of the liberty offered to workers through property ownership. Workers would increasingly find themselves squeezed towards subsistence level of existence.

The whole classical Marxian model of economic development reflects a failure to recognize the potential for innovation, for enhanced resource productivity, for expansion in income growth, that might act to keep any Malthusian forces in abeyance. It remains the case, however, that population growth did occur during early stages of industrial expansion, and that the early patterns of capitalist production did generate large urban concentrations which made separable individual units of real property impracticable for many participants in the inclusive production process. In relation to the analysis of this book, we may say that the guarantee of liberty afforded through property ownership was necessarily weakened, thereby making the viability of effective market competition more important in some relative sense. This conclusion holds even if the empirical record seems to have falsified the Malthusian prophecy, without which the whole classical Marxist model loses meaning.

In his last book, Hayek stressed the relationship between the productive efficiency of a market economy and the size of the population that can be sustained (1988). And he suggested that any revolutionary shift away from market institutions would, ultimately, ensure that population size be adjusted downwards. What Hayek fails to sense, however, is the relationship between the increasing market interdependence with its related increases in numbers of participants and the increasing difficulty that participants face in acquiring and holding property that might serve its traditional liberty-enhancing purpose. The modern urban man enjoys the fulsomeness of the highly-interdependent order of markets; but this person, at the same time, becomes increasingly dependent on the behaviour of others beyond any range of personal influence or control.

To an extent, this development is countered by the shift towards a post-industrial economic order, towards a service economy, which, as accompanied by the communication-information technological revolution, makes spatial concentration less necessary for the generation of economic value. The modern social problems do not lie in the Marxian proletariat, whose participants are property-less and subject to capitalist exploitation. The modern social problems, those that arise in the welfare-transfer state, are quite different, and, indeed, become almost the reverse of those sketched out by Marx. The modern urban underclass is not forced to levels of subsistence because wage levels are forced to the costs of reproduction of labour. The modern underclass does not produce value at all; transfer payments rather than wages become the source of living. And productive participants of economies are not likely to acquiesce in payments that enable non-producing recipients to accumulate property that will, to an extent, free them from dependency status. The urban underclass in the welfare-transfer state participates in the economy only as a consumer. The members of this class become the exploiters rather than the exploited; they secure *negative* surpluses; they use up value that they have no part in producing.

17. Final Speculations

Karl Marx understood neither the statics nor the dynamics of the capitalist economic order that he so persuasively criticized. Failing such understanding, Marx thought it necessary to replace the market order with some collectivist alternative that he understood even less. Nonetheless, we may interpret Marx as being acutely sensitive to the loss of liberty experienced by persons who shift into market-exchange relationships and away from the idyll of self-sufficient private, family or small community independence. In this sensibility, Marx joined one strand of classical political philosophy, Thomas Jefferson and the southern agrarians of this century, all of whom questioned the viability of a free society in the absence of peasant proprietorship, broadly defined.

We know, in 1992, that private ownership of property is necessary for efficiency in the production of economic value. We also know that extensive specialization is required in order for the scale economies of production to be realized. Individuals must concentrate their input capacities despite the knowledge that, in so doing, they increase their dependence on others beyond their own influence and control, either directly or indirectly. Even in complex modern economies, however, specialization need not be total. And through private ownership, persons may be able substantially to reduce their dependence on markets. Ownership of durables, including housing, allows space for own-production of a flow of services, hence alleviating any need for market purchase. In addition, private ownership of income-yielding assets allows adjustment of consumption-use patterns through time. These aspects of private ownership in modern Western economies remain significant, even if they are often overlooked. Only in the contrast with the pre-1989 socialist regimes do these liberty-enhancing qualities of property owner-ship come into full focus.

Nonetheless, even the complex web of interdependence that describes the modern economies of the United States, Japan and Western Europe seems far removed in its dimension of inde-pendence from the regime of yeoman farmers in Jefferson's idealized republic. Can measures be suggested that would main-tain or even increase the value productivity that extended spe-cialization makes possible and, at the same time, capture or recapture some of those attributes of independent existence that are universally valued in themselves?

The importance of monetary stabilization can scarcely be over-emphasized in this respect. Through its arbitrary authority to modify the exchange rate between money and goods, the nation-state, even in Western developed economies, reduces dramati-cally the potential protection that the citizen may secure through legally guaranteed holdings of property. The prospects for con-fiscation of value through monetary inflation reduce the intrinsic advantages of holding claims denominated in many and create a distortion in favour of real assets. An effective monetary consti-tution (which exists nowhere in the world) that would guarantee stability in the value of the monetary unit would, indeed, work miracles, whether measured against criteria of liberty or effi-ciency.

Monetary stability would also work to ensure that the macroeconomy function so as to prevent massive institutional failures akin to those experienced during the 1930s. Unemploy-ment arising from macroeconomic sources would be largely elimi-nated, thereby reducing the dependency status of all market participants.

A second major dimension that warrants notice here, even if the direction of effect is obvious, is that which measures the overall size of the politicized sector of economic life. To the extent that the individual is coercively subjected to taxes which, in turn, finance governmental programmes that presumably re-turn assigned shares in benefits, there is no available exit option. The argument from liberty, as advanced in this book, suggests that, even if the overall size of the politicized sector of the economy should be set precisely at some efficiency-enhancing optimum, the utility value of independence itself would dictate some reduction in public sector size.

As discussed earlier, the availability of alternative buyers and sellers in both input and output markets becomes more important as the economic unit shifts increasingly from the self-production afforded by property ownership towards dependence on market exchange. Competition in the market-place protects the individual from undue exploitation even when property-holdings are limited. But institutional structures can be adjusted so as to facilitate individuals' ability to exercise choices. Mobility among market options can be encouraged along many dimensions.

In a more general sense, the individual values private ownership that allows for a definition of a 'private sphere' of activity, even in the most interdependent of settings. Even the person who provides highly-specialized input services, and who depends for income on markets for such services, can remain at liberty in the choices that are made on buying sides of markets. There are exit options available in the modern competitive economy that are much more extensive than those faced by the yeoman farmer of Mr Jefferson's dreams. But the critically important linkage between market competition and individual liberty may not yet be fully sensed by those who continue to express preferences for asset ownership even when terms of trade seem unfavourable. Market forces may not be trusted for several reasons, including the lack of understanding of how these forces work. But, also, markets may be recognized to be vulnerable to interferences by politicians. *Laissez-faire*, as a policy stance, may be trusted more than its opposite. And individuals who feel too dependent on markets may seek greater protection for their residual liberties through structures of property ownership. But with modern jurisprudence on the legitimacy of governmental takings of privately-owned assets such security may be impossible to achieve.

The intricacies of the relationships between individual liberty and private property, analytically, empirically, historically and legally are surely deserving of critical attention. I do not claim to have done more than to scratch the surface of a research programme that remains largely undeveloped.

18. Endnote

The editor has strongly urged me to include explicit discussion of the implications of the above analysis for political organization and particularly for democratic institutions. The central argument is that private or several property serves as a guarantor of liberty, quite independently of how political or collective decisions are made. The direct implication is, of course, that effective constitutional limits must be present, limits that will effectively constrain overt political intrusions into rights of property, as legally defined, and into voluntary contractual arrangements involving transfer of property. If individual liberty is to be protected, such constitutional limits must be in place prior to and separately from any exercise of democratic governance.

An understanding of priorities in this respect should, of course, offer the basis for an extension of constitutional constraints on majoritarian legislative processes in modern polities and notably with reference to potential monetary and fiscal exploitation, quite apart from the more obvious 'takings' activity that must everywhere be condemned.

The omnipresent confusion that has corrupted Western attitudes and that threatens to close off the opportunities now presented to emerging post-socialist societies involves the failure to recognize that 'constitutional' must be placed in front of the word 'democracy' if the political equality of individuals is to be translated with any meaningful measure of freedom and autonomy. The tyranny of the majority is no less real than any other, and, indeed, it may be more dangerous because it feeds on the idealistic illusion that participation is all that matters.

References

Boswell, J. (1946), *The Journal of a Tour to the Hebrides with Samuel Johnson*, London: Everyman's Edition.

Buchanan, J.M. (1975), *The Limits of Liberty*, Chicago: University of Chicago Press.

Bush, W. (1972), 'Individual Welfare in Anarchy', in G. Tullock (ed.), *Explorations in the Theory of Anarchy*, The Public Choice Society Book and Monograph Series, Blacksburg, Va.: University Publications, pp. 5–18.

Hayek, F.A. (1988) *The Fatal Conceit: The Errors of Socialism*, Chicago: University of Chicago Press.

Hobbes, T. (1651), *Leviathan*, New York: Collier, 1962.

Pope Leo XIII (1939), *The Condition of Labor in Five Great Encyclicals*, ed. G.C. Treacy, New York: The Paulist Press, pp. 1–36 (*Rerum Novarum*).

Tullock, G. (ed.) (1972), *Explorations in the Theory of Anarchy*, The Public Choice Society Book and Monograph Series, Blacksburg, Va: University Publications.

Tullock, G. (1974), *The Social Dilemma; The Economics of War and Revolution*, The Public Choice Society Book and Monograph Series, Blacksburg, Va: University Publications.

Index